I Wasn't at the Library

Bernice Lipschultz Page

I Wasn't at the Library

Bernice Lipschultz Page

Mission Street Press
San Francisco, California

Copyright © 2014 Bernice Lipschultz Page. All rights reserved. No part of this book may be reproduced or transmitted in any form or by any means, electronic or mechanical, or by any information storage and retrieval systems, except in brief extracts for the purpose of review, without the written permission of the author.

Design JM Shubin,
Shubin Design (www.shubindesign.com).
Typefaces: Fairfield, Snell Roundhand

ISBN-978-0-9853672-9-2

First Edition/first Printing
Printed in the United States of America

Dedicated to my beloved daughter,
Bonnie

Red Flocked Wallpaper

Tessie and Morris Lipschultz.

February 6, 1923, was a gala day. I came into this beautiful world at Childrens' Hospital in San Francisco. Being the first child of my parents was quite an event; the celebration continued for two days!

Mom and Dad lived on McAllister Street until 1928, when the Cal Vets offered World War I veterans mortgages so they could purchase homes. Our house was on Munich Street in the Excelsior District, in the outer Mission. It was a two-bedroom home; I remember the red wine color of the flocked wallpaper in the front room. There was one bathroom, and yes, indoor plumbing.

On March 26, 1926, my brother Ken was born. Mom and dad were delighted to have another child. I was so proud when they placed him in my arms, like a new toy doll.

When I was five years old, I started kindergarten at the nearby Cleveland School. Neighbor kids who also attended Cleveland would walk to school and home—always with an adult at our sides, to make sure our trip was safe.

In 1929, when the Depression started, many neighbors—and my parents—lost their jobs and homes.

My father's parents had a wonderful business in San Francisco manufacturing men's caps. When it became evident in the Depression that they could no longer manage to keep the company, the factory was closed.

This started quite a bit of moving around, all of it in the Mission District. We started at the top of Rhode Island Street. The landlord raised the rent, so we had another move. This time it was three blocks down the hill to Vermont Street. That one was a large flat, with big rooms.

While living on Vermont Street, when I was six or seven years old, a man came by with his pony. It cost 25 cents for my brother Ken and I to have our picture taken on the pony.

I remember the man asked my mom if she would like to have me interviewed at the Dentyne company, as my teeth were so even. Mom said no, and that ended my modeling career.

Our next move was to Treat Avenue and 24th Street. Mom and Dad were separated, but they remained friends. They were both always there if we needed something. Our flat on 24th Street was an upstairs unit. I remember we had an icebox, and the iceman would deliver twice a week. The iceman wore a big leather protector on his shoulder and carried the heavy blocks of ice, held onto with huge prongs, up the stairs.

We didn't have a clothes washing machine. My mom had a washtub with a wringer attached to it. After washing and wringing out the clothes, she would go up to the roof and hang them on a line. When the clothes dried, Mom brought them down, ironed and folded them.

While living at the top of 24th Street, we had ball-bearing roller skates that attached to the bottoms of our shoes. We would skate from the top of Rhode Island down to Potrero Avenue, jumping the sidewalks onto the street, then jumping back onto the sidewalks. It was very daring! Those skates gave us many hours of fun.

The corner grocer was also wonderful, helping all the families with extra food. He went to the wholesaler daily. He had a horse and wagon, and filled the wagon up with fruit, vegetables, etc. All the mothers would be there awaiting his return, to buy the freshest items they could afford.

While in the deepest part of the Depression, various services and charities sent out trucks to all the neighborhoods, to make sure fruits and vegetables were delivered to as many people as possible.

One afternoon our doorbell rang, and Mom and I went downstairs to answer the door. A truck driver was standing there with a big box of very green apples. He offered an apple to my mother. She took one bite, spit it out and told the driver to leave with his green apples!

As he was leaving, Mom threw the apple at his back, yelling that no child of hers would ever eat those apples! We went back upstairs, thus ending our fruit deliveries by the charities.

On Sundays the children all went to St. Peter's Church. The sermons were in Latin, but we respectfully sat quietly until the service was over. Then we all went home, had lunch, and went outside to play games like hide and seek, hopscotch or kick the can.

Our family, and our neighbors, had very little money. We ate a lot of spaghetti covered with tomato soup. When we had an extra 20 cents or 25 cents, we would go to the butcher store and he would sell us hamburger. He also gave whoever went to the store, brother or sister, a hot dog or a piece of baloney.

The move had me changing schools, too. I started at Star King for grammar school, which was at 25th and Potrero. About a year later, Mom had me transferred to Bryant School, at 23rd and Bryant. That is where I graduated from 6th grade.

The best part of living on 24th Street in the early 1930s, as the Depression was ending, was that a fake Chinese laundry shop opened; it was actually a gambling hall. Mom and the neighbors had a wonderful time; the main game was keno at 10 cents a card. If you had a winning card, they delivered the winnings to your home, putting it through the mail slot.

I learned the game right away, and 80 years later, I am still doing my thing at the casinos ... playing strictly keno.

On many Sundays, Mom and Dad would take Ken and me to the Petaluma Park. We would drive onto the car ferry in San Francisco, and go to Sausalito on the auto boat. From there, we would take U.S. 101 to Petaluma.

Ken and I had wonderful times there, playing on the swings and slides. There was also a replica miniature horse to ride on.

Mom packed wonderful lunches for us. As we were always hungry in the fresh air, she made sure we had our bologna and cheese sandwiches, on white bread, and cookies.

The return to San Francisco was an adventure in itself. We would drive back down the highway to Sausalito, and then get in the bumper-to-bumper traffic on what was then Water Street. We'd finally get our turn to drive onto the ferry, and go back home.

Ken and I loved standing by the railing of the ferry, and watching the ocean beneath us.

Who ever dreamed that many years later, I would be living in Sausalito, on Glen Drive, looking down at what had been Water Street, and was now Caledonia Street? I could sit in my Sausalito home and remember the wonderful family days in Petaluma, and our happy times returning from Sausalito to San Francisco.

Playland at the Beach

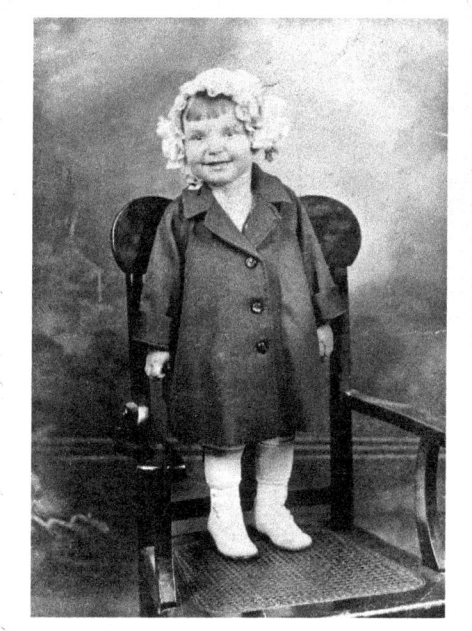

In the early 1930s, my dad had an Essex car. On weekends, he would take Ken and me to the Beach; this "beach" was really an amusement park called "Playland at the Beach," in San Francisco—right next to the Pacific Ocean.

Dad loved the European music played at the merry-go-round. He could sit for hours listening to it.

Ken and I would start our days on the merry-go-round. We would try to win a brass ring. The rings were placed on wooden poles, extended away from the merry-go-round. You would put your right arm out and try to get a finger into one of the rings. Then you'd grab it! If you were lucky enough to get a ring, you received a free ride on the merry-go-round. Once in a while, I was lucky enough to get a free ride.

Dad would give Ken and me some money for popcorn, then it was off to the Fun House, which Ken and I both loved. With the big Laughing Sally greeting us, we were excited to get into the Fun House and its many attractions.

As you went in, you walked by the Wall of Mirrors. These were not ordinary mirrors, and you could not believe what you saw in them. They made you look too tall, or too fat, or too thin. They were scary, but a lot of fun.

Then Ken and I went to The Barrel of Laughs. This was a 6-foot round item, which was meant to be a barrel on its side. The barrel was always turning slowly, and you had to walk through it without falling.

I loved the indoor slides at the Funhouse. You went down them on a burlap sack, so you would not hurt your tushy as you slid down the slide's 200 feet.

Ken loved the Joy Wheel. That was a flat surface that continuously spun around. It was at least ten feet in diameter, and you had to try and stay in the middle of the wheel without sliding off.

The Beach also had many wonderful rides, such as Shoot the Chutes—a speed boat-themed roller coaster ride. Your "boat" would travel to the top of the rails and zoom down to the water below. What a scare, but what fun, as you held on for dear life! There was a roller skating rink too, and we spent many happy hours there.

We also had games of chance to play and win prizes. At 25 cents per game, one of my favorites was throwing darts at inflated balloons, in an attempt to burst them. If you won, you would receive a stuffed animal. If you wanted, you could also get a balloon.

There were many places to eat at The Beach; did you know the It's It ice cream treat was invented there? One famous restaurant and nightclub was Topsy's Roost. The older crowd loved the nightclub, but we were too young, and not allowed in.

Other places served hot dogs, hamburgers, tamales and enchiladas, among other things. We all ate very well.

Our times there were the happiest days of our young lives.

Many years later, Playland at the Beach was torn down completely, and condos and homes were built on the land. Believe me, it was the saddest of times when we'd drive by there and see them demolishing the Playland facilities.

To stop our sadness, we'd go to the Cliff House Restaurant for a meal. The food was good, but it signaled the end of our visits to Playland at the Beach.

"I Smoke Now"

In September, 1933, my parents had another baby, and named him William. Our flat on 24th Street was a little full, but there was always room for one more.

In 1933, when I was 10 years old, my girlfriends Vera, Barbara, Dorothy, and I had just enough money to go to the Mission St. theater called the El Capitan. Outside the theater was a candy and cigarette counter. We four girls, Barbara, Vera, Dorothy and I, each had a nickel, so we put our money together to buy cigarettes, which were ten cents a pack. We discussed what brand we would try, and Chesterfields was the winner. We went into the show and sat in the balcony. We each took a cigarette, lit it, and inhaled. One of the girls coughed, but the other girls and I inhaled and loved it! What a wonderful afternoon.

When I got home that day, my mom and dad were in the living room, listening to the radio. I walked in, looked at them, and said, "I smoke now. I can't afford to buy them, but they're reasonable, and you can take care of that."

When they got over their shock, they started telling me of all the dangers. In one ear, and out the other. My dad smoked King Optimo cigars. He brought one to me, and said, "Inhale this." No cough came out of me!

I smoked until I was 82 years old, and enjoyed every cigarette.

In the '30s my dad found a wonderful outdoor Chinese tobacco store, which sold Chinese strips of coconut in little paper bags. The bags were 10 cents each. Dad would buy each of us a bag.

Then we would go for a little ride down Stockton Street to Market Street. We'd go up Market to 18th Street, turn left and head back to 24th Street.

Growing up on 24th was quite an adventure. We had Harrison Park at 25th and Treat Avenue where we could play.

Every week or so, one of the neighborhood kids would fall down and break an arm or a leg and immediately go to the hospital. Our hospital was San Francisco General, located on Potrero Avenue between 22nd and 23rd. The emergency room was always full of kids, including me.

In 1933, I was out playing when all of a sudden, down I went on my completely curled up left arm. It hurt quite a bit, so off to the hospital for me. In those days we took the streetcar to 24th and Potrero, and walked one block to the hospital.

At the emergency room the doctor sent me to have my arm x-rayed. I had a compound fracture of my left arm, and was fitted with a plaster of Paris cast to keep my arm in place.

When I got back home and my friends saw the cast, they all wanted to sign it. I wore the cast for a month due to the severity of the break.

As my brother Bill grew up, he became an all-around game player on 24th Street. He played all the games that boys of that era enjoyed. One day, when Bill was six or seven years old, he and the Huff Brothers went to Harrison Park at 25th and Treat. At the time, Superman was popular, as he flew through the sky.

Bill climbed a tree at the park. He lifted his arms as if they were wings, and jumped—just as Superman would! Of course, Bill landed face down, and knocked himself out. One arm was broken, and he was bruised all over.

His friends walked him home. Our mom took one look at Bill, and smacked him for climbing the tree. Mom then walked Billy to the emergency room at San Francisco General Hospital. He had to get lots of stitches, especially to his face and forehead.

They walked back home, and Bill had to stay in bed for a week.

Between Bill and me, there was never a dull moment ... and there were many visits to the emergency room!

Pools and Schools

In 1935 I joined the Girl Scouts. My troop met at the Good Samaritan Center at 25th and Potrero Avenue-, and our leader's name was Oriole. One field trip that my troop went on was to the Fairmont Hotel on top of Nob Hill in San Francisco. We went there to swim in the Tonga Room. Can you imagine the beauty and luxury of the hotel and its lobby, which my troop admired that day? After a fun-filled afternoon, we went to the restaurant in the hotel for a little refreshment. This was one of the happiest days of my life. I'm sure that all the troop members felt the same way.

Many years later, I was on a date at the Fairmont Hotel. I was dressed in a beautiful gown and lovely jewelry. As we arrived, my mind went back to that day when the Girl Scouts went for an afternoon swim.

This evening our table was at the edge of the pool, and I could see my youthful self in the pool. There was a raft floating in the pool, which the orchestra was on. We danced alongside the pool as the band played beautiful music; It was a wonderful evening to remember.

Upon graduation from 6th grade, I enrolled in Horace Mann Jr. High. It was quite a change from grammar school. I even had a homeroom, with Miss Mahoney as my homeroom teacher.

My first class was an introduction to the language teacher, Miss Biddle; she said we had a choice of three languages to study—Spanish, Italian and French. I chose Spanish, as did my girlfriends.

During our summer vacation from school, we were very fortunate to have a beautiful swimming pool in the neighborhood; it was called the "Nickel Bath," and was at 19th and Guerrero streets. This was an indoor pool run by the City of San Francisco.

One nickel rented us a bathing suit and a towel. The pool, dressing rooms, and surrounding area were immaculate. Lifeguards were always on duty. Kids from 24th Street were there en masse, enjoying every minute!

After outgrowing the Nickel Baths, we were allowed to go swimming at Sutro Baths. This was a large, privately owned building at Land's End, right next to the Pacific Ocean. It housed many pools, with water ranging from warm to cold. We would take a streetcar directly there from 24th and Mission.

The price for a day at the Sutro Baths was 25 cents. For that we received a wool bathing suit and a towel. There was a narrow opening for each dressing room. We'd change in there, and go take a quick shower before heading to the pools.

Sutro Baths was just as immaculate as the Nickel Baths.

When those wool swim suits got wet ... they stretched out. We girls sure had our problems holding them up while we were in the water, but we survived!

We all enjoyed 7th, 8th and 9th grades. At our graduation we were allowed to enroll in any high school we wished. I picked the High School of Commerce, which was at the foot of Van Ness Avenue.

I Wasn't at the Library

My senior photo from Commerce High School.

In May, 1937, the Golden Gate Bridge was opened. School was closed for the big event. Vera, Dorothy, Barbara, Andrew, John and I arrived at the bridge and walked across it, admiring the incredible views. There was no auto traffic on the bridge that beautiful day.

We brought our lunches and sat on the Marin side of the bridge to eat. We marveled at the Marin Headlands and the new bridge that could take you to Marin County. It was not overly crowded. Everyone enjoyed themselves, walking leisurely in both directions on the bridge.

We arrived back home about 4 p.m., proud to be in the first group of people to walk across the Golden Gate Bridge!

Commerce was a co-ed school. The school centered on business skills, and our football team was great. While I was studying typing and shorthand, our team, the Bulldogs, were competing against Mission High and the other SF schools for the City Championship. As I recall, we did win it a few times.

To get to high school, we walked to Potrero Avenue and took the H streetcar to and from there. The fare was 5 cents each way. The conductor and the operator were always well dressed in railroad-type uniforms. They had railroad pocket watches and made sure we were always on time.

In 1937, when I was only 14 years old, Dad purchased a '37 Plymouth, and immediately started teaching me to drive. There was a big empty lot at 25th and Potrero, where we practiced for quite a while…"low, second, high, reverse"…changing gears with the car's stickshift.

I was a quick learner, soon driving around our area. I remember driving just to Mission Street, returning on 24th; that was my limit.

While attending Commerce High School, Vera, Barbara and I thought we'd like to go to Wolohans Dance Palace at 10th and Market. We told our moms we were going to the library. On Fridays, we would go dancing, leaving the dance hall about 9 p.m. to take a jitney to 24th, and continue home.

These dances had live bands, a bar where you could buy sodas or alcoholic drinks, and people of all ages to enjoy the evening with. During one visit to the dance hall, when I was 15, Miss O'Sullivan, the San Francisco Police Department's Juvenile Officer, was there on duty. Guess who she stopped? Me!

She asked me how old I was. I smiled and said, "18." That went over like a lead balloon, and I had to give her my name and phone number. Officer O'Sullivan called my mom, and visited her within a few days. She explained we were under-age and forbidden to go to a public dance hall. Mom thanked Officer O'Sullivan very much.

When I got home from school, Mom let me know who was boss! She whacked me, and said there would be no more library.

Mentally, I started planning my life after I turned 18.

Our junior year of high school arrived. At the foot of Van Ness Avenue there was an ice cream/soda fountain. After school we would go there to have a Coke and a smoke. That was really Big Time!

We had our physical education classes in a large field across Van Ness Avenue from Commerce High School. While we had PE, the ROTC trained along the outer edge of the field. That field has since become an auditorium for plays, musicals, etc. You may have heard of the auditorium—it is Davies Symphony Hall!

My senior year arrived, and I had become very proficient in business office procedures such as shorthand and typing. The school had a work program, and students were hired by stores in the area. I worked at Hale Bros. Department Store, and Kress 5 and 10 Cent Store at 5th and Market Streets. Although sales didn't require my use of shorthand, it did pay me ten cents per hour!

I also planned for after my graduation, which was to be January, 1941. My goal was to get a job in the business sector. My graduation from Commerce High School was quite the event for my family. I am the oldest of my siblings, and my finishing high school provided a good role model for them. My graduation gown was the school's blue and gold colors. The caps were blue, and our tassels were gold. The ceremony was in the school auditorium.

After graduation, I signed on with an employment agency that specialized in temporary help; I was lucky enough to always get a job in the Financial District of San Francisco.

November 1953 — Working the livestock show at the Cow Palace. The Seals uniform sure got around.

My Early Careers

Who ever dreamt that a world war would draw the United States into it, in December, 1941? On December 8, 1941, one day after the attack on Pearl Harbor, my dad escorted me to the personnel office at Fort Mason.

I took typing and shorthand tests, and was hired immediately by the Army's personnel department. I worked from 3 p.m. to 11 p.m. Sometimes I worked at Pier 37, typing and keeping the records of the supplies being placed on the troop ships.

I was still dancing, too! I loved to dance at El Patio, Wolohans and the Avalon Ballroom. Now I was legal to be dancing, and there were many appreciative GIs there—we all enjoyed every minute.

The Federal Government soon started the Office of Price Administration; this was the agency that made sure there was no price gouging. All department stores, retailers, grocers, auto shops, gas stations, etc., were constantly checked to make sure they were keeping their pricing records in line with the administrative orders issued to make sure citizens could buy needed items. When I started there, I was the chief secretary in the legal department.

In 1942, Mom had a baby girl named Helen, and in 1943, Mom had another baby boy, named Stanley. They were quite a surprise, but we all managed to live together on 24th Street.

I spent twenty years as a Government employee, transferring to the various agencies as needed.

Around 1947, while working at the Office of Price Stabilization, I worked with a lady named Ann. She asked if I would be interested in becoming an usherette—working at Winterland, the Cow Palace, Seals Stadium, etc. Ann was already an usherette, and thought I would like a second job also.

I jumped at that idea! I worked as an usherette until 1958; I retired after working the opening day of Major League Baseball on the West Coast—the San Francisco Giants hosted the Los Angeles Dodgers at Seals Stadium, and I was working the seating area behind home plate!

For years I worked the wrestling events at Winterland, stationed down front. It was the time of Gorgeous George. I was there to ensure that fans were in the correct seats. The famous stars Max Baer and Johnnie Weissmuller were frequent visitors. Winterland also hosted the Ice Follies, which, of course, I ushered! We also worked at the Cow Palace, which hosted rodeos, entertainers, movie stars, and more.

Ushering days at Winterland.

Forming a Team

Another lovely lady I worked with at OPA was Pauline Pearce. We became friends, and she introduced me to her boyfriend, who turned out to be the famous local sportswriter Jack Rosenbaum. The three of us hit it off immediately.

Jack always gave us passes to the horse races, theaters, dinners and many social events. We had the time of our lives.

In June, 1944, Jack met us for lunch, and informed us that some entrepreneurs in San Francisco were going to form a pro football team; the meeting was held at the St. Francis Candy Shop on 24th Street.

Jack asked if we would be available to assist in starting the team's office; we were delighted to be of service! Airline tickets, appointments, etc., were always part of this new job, which kept me busy nights and weekends when I wasn't ushering.

Players and coaches, including Buck Shaw, Frankie Albert, and Bruno Banducci were always coming into the office.

You now know the team as the five-time Super Bowl Champion San Francisco 49ers.

Three Months Later We Were Eloping to Yosemite

On New Year's Eve, 1944, I was at home, waiting for my date. When the bell rang, I answered the door—standing there was this big hunk that I had never met before.

I asked, "Who are you?" He tried to make up some silly thing. I ignored him, as my date arrived, and off we went. Turns out he was "Mom's" son Joe; Mom was our housecleaner.

The next day my mom said that Joe would like to see me again. I told my mom I'd think about it. Well, I broke down and started dating him. Three months later we were eloping to Reno, and honeymooning in Yosemite.

Joe and I lived in an apartment on Clay and Scott Streets for five years. In September, 1950, we had a baby girl, Kathy. When I was home caring for her, Jack Rosenbaum would come by, telling me it was pleasant at my house, and that he enjoyed my friendship. We'd have a cup of coffee, and then he'd be off to his next reporting assignment!

Soon after, Joe and I divorced. I went to live with my mom on 24th Street, and returned to work.

In 1952, Kathy started attending the Holy Family Day Home, which was in San Francisco at 16th and Guerrero. I was on leave from my government position, and I went to work for the law firm of Tobriner and Lazarus located in the Russ Building in San Francisco, handling various secretarial duties.

One job I had there was assisting with the paperwork for the projects of the American Federation of Labor (AFL). Many people were in and out of the office during this time, including the movie star Melvin Douglas and his wife Helen Gahagan Douglas. Mr. Douglas was a very quiet gentleman, but he was always there to participate in the formation meetings.

Me Looking Snazzy— 1954.

Alaska–"Uncharted Territory"

Everyone who worked at Ladd Air Force Base was issued this informative booklet.

In 1955, the AFL's business was completed and I returned to work for the government.

During the time Kathy was at Holy Family Day Home, in 1955, I, of course, dropped her off and picked her up. Also there with her children was a lovely lady named DeAnne. She was a photographer, and was planning to go to Alaska to continue her career. She asked if I would like to go with her.

My heart pounded! I told her I would love to! That was even before Alaska was a state.

My mother and friends could not believe that I would leave

San Francisco for such a faraway place. DeAnne left a few weeks ahead of me, and I joined her in Fairbanks soon after; I roomed with her for almost a month, until I got my feet on the ground.

The adventure started with my flight up to Fairbanks. While en route, the pilot announced we were flying over "uncharted territory." All the passengers gasped, and I said to myself, "I am too young for this."

I discovered that life in Fairbanks was very different than what I'd known. The town was out of an old cowboy movie—the roads were dirt and the sidewalks were wooden. Of course, there were bars galore.

I applied for a job at Ladd Air Force Base, and immediately was hired as a civilian secretary. I moved to the base housing, as it was easier to be close to my job.

A movie called "The Spoilers" was being filmed in Fairbanks, with Rory Calhoun in a main role. As DeAnne was the local newspaper's photographer, she was assigned to take photos when the shooting was at an indoor setting.

I went along with DeAnne, and then on to a bar called Club Rendezvous where I met Rory. I asked him where he was from; when he told me he was from Santa Cruz, I told him I was from San Francisco, and wondered aloud to him what were we doing up here at the top of the world. He smiled, and was called back to the movie.

When the filming was over, all the movie stars went back to Hollywood.

As civilians in Alaska, we had telephone service on Tuesdays and Thursdays at the Army office on Main Street. The first call I made was to my mother, asking her to send me knee-high boots, and to contact my dentist to find out what type of toothpaste to buy! I didn't want my teeth to get yellow like the teeth of the "sourdoughs" (that's what the old-timers there were called).

The package that came from home had my new boots and a box of baking soda in it.

On weekends, DeAnne and I would go to the Club Rendezvous. We had wonderful times there. We met many handsome men and were always being taken out on dates.

There was so much to see, such as abandoned gold mines, mountains, beautiful lakes, and a trip to the North Pole! Well, the "North Pole" was a town that had a post office and received Santa's mail.

At the same time I was in Alaska, my brother Bill was in the Army, and stationed at Fort Lewis, Washington; that was near Tacoma. One weekend I flew down to be with him. We had a great time—we went to the G I's bar and met his buddies, then we went to the downtown area.

Bill's girlfriend Sue was waiting, as she worked in the area. She smiled as we arrived, then came and sat in the car with us. Bill introduced me to the lady who would be my future sister-in-law!

Bill is so lucky to have Sue. They have been together more than 55 years, and are still "young lovers."

My Phone Number was on the Note

One night after my return to San Francisco in 1955, I was on a date. The guy's car had broken down, so we used mine to go downtown. As we were going to a dinner and show, I parked in an open parking lot next to Joe's Restaurant.

Wouldn't you know … when we got back to my car, it wouldn't start. I left a note on the car, telling the attendant to please not tow the car, as I would be there early in the morning. When I arrived back at the lot in the morning and saw the attendant, my heart skipped a beat!

We started talking, and the attendant asked if he could see me sometime. I picked up the note from my car (my phone number was on the note) and handed it to him. I said that if he wanted to see me, he now had my phone number.

He was George Farish. A day or so later, George did call me, and a new romance developed.

Six months later we were married at City Hall in San Francisco. We moved into a lovely apartment on 20th at Howard Street.

Later, George lost his job and become morose. He would go out, stay out late and have a few drinks. I had Kathy with me, and his actions were becoming too much of a burden.

We parted, and I left for Reno for a divorce. The laws were not very restrictive; I only had to be a resident of Nevada for six weeks to obtain a divorce. Kathy stayed with my mother.

I had flown to Reno. When I arrived I hailed a cab, and told the driver to take me to a boarding house. I was very lucky, as the cab driver knew of a house with rooms for rent. The next day I applied for work at the Nevada Club. What a time I had as a change girl! I worked from 1 a.m. to 9 a.m.

At some point, my mom brought Kathy up to see me. My landlady also had a room for them. At the same time, Bill and Sue came to visit, and the landlady had a room for them.

While everyone was there, Bill and Sue decided they wanted to go gamble ... however, Sue wasn't 21 years old yet. She went to the Nevada Club and was caught by security.

Bill and Sue went back to the rooming house, where Sue borrowed one of my "grown up" blouses, a pair of my shoes, and a little make-up. Suddenly she looked older. They returned to the club and nobody bothered them for the rest of the weekend.

After my six weeks there, my attorney in Reno, recommended by an associate in San Francisco, went to court with me. The landlady was my witness to having never left the state during the six weeks. My divorce from George was granted.

A Meeting at John's Rendezvous

I returned to San Francisco and rented an apartment on Valencia at 18th Street; Kathy was with me. I would drop her off and pick her up, at the Holy Family Day Home's babysitting service. When I had an ushering job, my mom would take Kathy for the night and get her back to school the next morning.

Kathy went to grade school on Dolores Street. After school, she and other students were escorted back to Holy Family Day Home. Helen would pick Kathy up later, and bring her home for the day.

It was during this time that my mom moved to the outer Mission area of San Francisco, leaving 24th Street after all those years. Helen and Stan moved with her, and Kathy and I joined them in the new house. Ken had married, and was living in the Los Angeles area, and Bill was in the Army.

By then I was employed at the General Services Administration in San Francisco. The GSA was in charge of purchasing for federal agencies.

On Friday nights, when the San Francisco Seals minor league baseball team was in town, my dad and I would meet for dinner. Dad was working at the Marine Corps Building on lower Mission Street as a security officer. We liked to go to a restaurant named John's Rendezvous. After dinner I would get the #25 bus at 5th and Market, and go directly to Seals Stadium for my usherette job.

One particular evening, Dad and I were eating when I looked over his shoulder. A handsome man was sitting there, eating a sandwich and pretending he wasn't looking at me. Of course, this was the era when we girls were always dressed in our working uniforms and wore our makeup. I was a blond then, with my jewelry shining.

Dad excused himself from the table, and the other gentleman kept looking at me. So I said, "Is that a good roast beef sandwich?" He shyly answered, "Its ham."

I smiled and asked if he were off to have a good time somewhere. "No," he said, he was off to a math class at the Monadnock Building. I casually mentioned that I was an usherette at Seals Stadium, and was leaving for my night job there.

My dad came back, took me to the bus, and off to work I went.

The next Friday came around, and my dad asked me if I wanted to go to John's for dinner. I said, "Of course. Let's see if that cute fellow comes in."

Lo and behold, ten minutes after we got to the restaurant, that cute fellow did come in! He picked up his order, and sort of hesitated by our table. I asked if he would like to join us, and he sat right down!

We started chatting. He mentioned that he had gone to Seals Stadium last Saturday, but I wasn't there. I told him that I had a daughter, and she had dance lessons on Saturday mornings.

The gentleman then told us his name was Tom Page, and he worked for Greyhound Bus Lines. Tom asked if he could see me, and I told him he had to ask my dad. He did ask, and Dad said, "Of course, if Bea wants to." I gave him my phone number, and he called that week.

The next weekend Tom and I had a date. We went to El Patio. We had fun! During the date, Tom told me about the wounds he still had from his WWII Army time; he made the battles sound like a job that just had to be done. He went on to say he had been in and out of the Army hospitals for four years. He had received two Purple Hearts for service in the Battle of the Bulge. After that, he rarely spoke of his war stories again.

Las Vegas—The Wee Kirk of the Heather Chapel

Tom and I in Santa Cruz
July 1957 (with Kathy hiding behind).

Tom's brother Cliff was in the Air Force, and my brother Bill was in the Army. We were a very proud family.

Tom and Kathy were wonderful together. One winter day we went beyond Sacramento to play in the snow. Tom and Kathy rode snow saucers down the hill and had snowball fights.

While Tom was courting me, he wanted me to meet his parents; I told him I would be delighted to. This was still during the baseball season and the next Saturday, while I was ushering the seats behind home plate at Seals Stadium, Tom and his mother Vera came up the aisle to me. The first two things I noticed were the funny hat she had on and her beautiful brown eyes.

I hugged her and told her I was delighted to meet her. I had procured some nearby seats, and escorted them over to the good seats. Tom's father Cliff was a chief engineer on the Northwestern Pacific Railroad. He was not a baseball fan, and didn't come to the stadium that day.

A week after I met Vera, Tom invited me to dinner at his parents' home in Sausalito. That's where I met Cliff. He came off as brusk, but kind.

One night we were at my mom's house with Helen, Stan and Kathy. Out of the blue Tom asked me to marry him. I said, "Yes"! We found an apartment on 18th Street at Dolores, across from Dolores Park. Then Tom and I drove to Las Vegas and were married in the Wee Kirk of the Heather Chapel on November 15, 1957,

In February, 1958, I invited Mom and Dad (as I called Vera and Cliff), to dinner at our place, to celebrate my birthday. I had arranged for a real Jewish dinner ... bagels, lox, pickles, corned beef and birthday cake.

While we were dining, the telephone rang. It was Tom's brother Cliff announcing that he had just become the proud father of a baby boy! My father-in-law jumped up, grabbed Vera, and said they had to get down to Cliff's family at Edwards Air Force Base.

Off they went, and left us sitting there with all that food.

Sausalito and the In-Laws

Meeting my future mother-in-law Vera at Seals Stadium. Note the funny hat.

Before the start of the 1958 baseball season, which, incidentally, was the year the Giants and the Dodgers moved to the west coast, we were in the apartment in San Francisco. Vera and Cliff came over one day, and asked Tom and me if we would like to take over their home on Glen Drive, in Sausalito. They had retired, and wanted to travel the world; they bought a trailer to start their adventures.

We were thrilled, and moved into the Sausalito house. With the long commute that brought, I decided to retire from my ushering career. My last day to usher was the West Coast debut of Major League Baseball—the opening day game between the Los Angeles Dodgers and the San Francisco Giants.

When my in-laws returned from their journeys they lived in their trailer at a mobile home park in Larkspur, California.

Dad's (I called my father-in-law Cliff "Dad"), favorite trip was anywhere there was a rodeo. They would drive up and down the coast, including Canada and Mexico, to see a rodeo; even a venture to the Nevada desert wasn't out of the question if the show was going to be good.

When I was still an usherette, I had worked the yearly rodeo at the Cow Palace. Dad was my guest to see the shows, and he loved it. He would walk around the barns and the back area, saying "Hi" to the many friends he met in the rodeo world.

Dad introduced me to the entertainer Slim Pickens. At this time, Slim was a rodeo clown; he was always very nice. He later became a movie star, and through the years I saw him portraying a cowboy in many movies.

In 1959 the roller derby came to San Francisco. Dad told me he loved the action, and would love to see it in person. I mentioned that one very famous skater, Ann Jensen, was a dear friend of mine; we had grown up together on 24th Street.

Dad was thrilled, and off we went to the roller derby match at the Cow Palace. When the game started, the fans went crazy—the screaming was incredible!

At intermission, I took Dad down to the rink, and introduced him to "Big Red," as Ann was known. We chatted for a while, and went back to our seats. Dad was so pleased to have met her.

During the second half of the match, the fans' cheering was even stronger. I was pregnant with Bonnie at the time—due in a few weeks—and the cheering seemed to go directly to my stomach, which was heaving and turning. I thought the baby might come into the world that night but luckily she held off until the end of August.

Big Bonnie

Kathy and Tom with a young Bonnie.

During my time at the OPA I met Bonnie Riley and we became fast friends. She lived in the North Beach area of San Francisco; we had many Italian dinners together in the wonderful restaurants in North Beach.

Bonnie was a tall, slender Irish lady with big blue eyes. Her hair was long and blond, and she had the best Irish wit of anyone I've ever known. She had a sister who lived nearby and was married to a doctor for the Board of Health in San Francisco. Bonnie's sister frequently joined us for dinners.

Eventually Bonnie transferred to Reno, but I did not want to forget her, so my baby girl, born in August, 1959, was named Bonnie Theresa; Bonnie for my dear Bonnie Riley, and Theresa after my mother.

In the mid-1960s we took a family vacation to Reno. I called "Big Bonnie" and told her which hotel we were staying at. A day or so later Bonnie came over with a gentleman who was shorter than she was by five inches! I hugged Bonnie and asked who the man was. She whispered, "My husband. Were you expecting Ramon Navarro?"

That set the tone for a great visit with Bonnie and her husband.

Losing Parents

In 1961, my father passed away. He had taken ill, and died at the Fort Miley hospital in San Francisco.

My mother was to join him on Christmas morning, December 25, 1965.

Am I a Bingo Player?

As all good women have done through the years, I looked for a hair salon in my new hometown. It became especially important one day, as Tom and I were supposed to go to the Fairmont Hotel for dinner and dancing that evening.

Tom got a sore throat, and I had a feeling we wouldn't be going out that night, but I kept my salon appointment, and "got beautiful."

At the salon, in the chair next to me, was a lovely red-headed lady. She smiled and asked if I was a new resident in Sausalito. She asked my name, and was pleasantly surprised that I was a "Page." This nice woman was Mae Burkell, the wife of the founder of the long-standing Sausalito business Burkell Plumbing. She knew my in-laws quite well.

Mae asked if I were a bingo player. "In California?" was my response; I thought the gambling was left in Nevada. Mae told me that the local bingo game was at the Star of the Sea Catholic Church, every Tuesday night; she wondered if I might want to go with her.

Who could say no? The church was just around the corner from our house. I now had Mae's phone number, and an invitation to play bingo. I went home from the salon with my new hairdo, and new friend's number; I told Tom that Mae had invited me to the Tuesday bingo, and he said, "Go ahead."

I called Mae and told her I would pick her up; Mae never did learn to drive. The first night at the Star of the Sea bingo, I lost ten dollars. However, that did start my gambling career in Sausalito.

The next day my dad was visiting us. I told him I'd lost at bingo the night before. He looked at me, gave me the money, and said, "If you can't afford it, don't go!"

Soon Mae and I were going to Reno on the Greyhound bus. We'd take $30 or $35, and play the nickel slot machines. The payoffs were $7.50! When we won, we were thrilled!

Once-a-month trips to Reno turned into twice-a-month trips. We were still playing Star of the Sea Tuesday night bingo, and had added Friday night bingo at the Sausalito Portuguese Hall.

On Friday nights there was always a whist (card game) scheduled before the bingo game. Tom would be there, front and center, playing whist, when I arrived for bingo.

Busy Bea Times

Sue Green, Mae Burkell, Ada Andre, and me at Finocchio's.

In the mid-1960s Tom took a Civil Service test, to be an accountant for the US Government. He passed with flying colors, and was soon working at the US Mint in San Francisco.

In 1969, my father-in-law, Clifford, became ill. In a short time, he passed away. That left my mother-in-law, Vera, living alone in her trailer at the mobile home park in Larkspur.

Kathy went to live with Vera. Also living in that park, with his stepfather, was Rodney Lasater. Kathy and Rodney became friends, and that turned into a romance. They were soon married. After living in

Vallejo for a short time, they moved to Oklahoma, where Rodney had grown up. A daughter and son later, they are still married and going strong.

During 1970, Vera became ill. She moved to the old Cottage Hospital site, now a convalescent home, in San Rafael. Despite the wonderful care, Vera passed away later in the year.

Another bingo friend of mine was Ada Andre. She was a waitress her whole life; when I knew her, she was working at a small local restaurant on Bridgeway in Sausalito. Ada was always ready for a gambling trip or a night out.

Mae, Ada and I met Sue Green at bingo in the 1970s. Sue's husband owned a successful auto parts store at 10th and Howard in San Francisco. Sue loved to entertain, and would often invite us out. We loved to go to Finnochio's, a nightclub in North Beach where the "female" entertainers were really men in drag.

Another bingo buddy was Hank De Miola. He lived up the hill from us on Glen Drive in Sausalito. Hank turned into a good friend, showing up at our house with birthday cakes for Kathy and Bonnie, or stopping by to help with chopping down trees and gardening.

Hank lived with his partner Carol, who did not like gambling. Hank would meet us in Reno and sleep in his car, while the rest of us, who had gone there on Greyhound, would stay at the Nugget Hotel. We'd all meet up at the Nugget, and gambled together.

My first Bea's Corner in Mill Valley.

Bea's Corner

Me and Santa Claus at my San Rafael store.

In 1974, after Kathy had married and while Bonnie was attending Tamalpais High School in Mill Valley, I decided to open a store.

I set up shop in Mill Valley at a little shopping area known as The Port, and called my store Bea's Corner. As that is where Bonnie's high school was, I had immediate customers. (Tom and Kathy had also gone to Tam.).

I sold clothing, jewelry and knickknacks. As sales increased, I made the decision to expand, and Bea's Corner moved to San Rafael! The store was in a busy shopping neighborhood. A local newspaper called The Newspointer ran an article about me and the store, which brought many new customers!

In 1981 I knew it was time to retire, and leave my sales career as a success. I had a huge going-out-of-business sale. People bought everything, including the fixtures.

When Bonnie was about 14, and attending Tamalpais High School, she informed Tom and me that she was going to join the Mill Valley Police Department's Explorer Program, with the hopes of eventually becoming a police officer.

After Tom and I calmed down, I asked her if she wouldn't want to be a stewardess. "No," she said, adding that they are just "glorified waitresses." Would she like to be a school teacher like her aunt and uncle? "No."

Bonnie gave the same response at the suggestion of becoming a legal secretary.

After all the "no's" we heard, we decided to help her all the way with her education to become a police officer. Bonnie graduated from Tam, and went on to the College of Marin to study Administration of Justice.

Between the ages of 18 and 21, Bonnie worked at the San Rafael, Fairfax, and Sausalito police departments. Bonnie was a cadet, a meter maid and reserve police officer.

In June, 1981, she was hired as an officer at the Twin Cities Police Department!

The Tiffany's of the Canal

Published June 10, 1981, East San Rafael newspaper
By Brad Breithaupt

Bea Page, the energetic proprietress of East San Rafael's knicknack nook, Bea's Corner, laughingly calls her store "The Tiffany's of the Canal."

She's proud of the merchandise that she offers to her customers, many of whom have been loyal visitors to her Belvedere Street Store since she moved in five years ago.

Tucked into a corner near Sil's Market, her store is a potpourri. She sells everything from "excellent fake" gold rings for $3.75 each to an already well-hugged Cookie Monster.

She is particularly proud of the clothing she carries. From the latest in ladies' blouses and skirts to used outfits, she meets her customers' tastes. Whether it be elegance, already worn-in or funk, Bea's got it.

She points to some new summer blouses that she's marked for $14.75. The same blouses are being sold at major department stores for $25, she says.

The key to her store's success? "When I get a good buy, you get a good buy," Bea firmly states. "In my store I sell them at what they should be," she says, pointing to a shelf of knick-nacks that she's selling for $2 apiece.

A former legal secretary for the U.S. Internal Revenue service, Bea decided seven years ago to slow down from her 100-word per minute typing and 180 words per minute shorthand. "I could not pound that typewriter one more minute," she admits.

Recognizing that most of her clientel don't fit the Marin County image of free-flowing wealth, she says she buys her merchandise with its affordability in mind.

Selling used clothes, she notes that many of her customerss prefer used apparel. "They say it feels softer," she states. "What does Magnin's have that I don't?" she jokingly boasts.

If the question was rephrased, "What do I have that Magnin's doesn't?" the most apparent answer would be Bea, herself.

She's having the time of her life running the store. Bea says it's her customers that keep her going.

Her store is crowed, overall her

merchandise doesn't exactly match Gump's elegance and her store's layout wasn't the work of a high-priced interior decorator, but it has Bea, a dynamo saleswoman who knows what her customers want and what they can afford.

Apparently her customers appreciate her awareness of their needs. "I take an interest in what they buy. If it doesn't fit right I tell them."

Holding up a new arrival—denim halters decorated with studs and rhinestones which she marks for $5 apiece, she proudly states, "I love every customer that comes in the door"

Bea is proud that her store carries less expensive merchandise. One advantage, she admits, is that should a customer break something accidentally, she doesn't have to worry about it.

She points to a handwritten sign behind the counter, "A broken item will never replace a valued customer."

Not having to worry about expensive Waterford crystal being modeled on a fragile shelf is a welcomed relief to Bea. Most of her items cost $1–$2, and both Bea and her customers like it that way.

Tom Passed Away

Dressing up on my cruise to Alaska in 1996 with Char.

In late 1981, I was hired by the Sausalito Police Department to coordinate the crime prevention and neighborhood watch programs. Both programs were a success. I coordinated the volunteers who did our department's presentations in homes and businesses. I was also called on to assist the department with mail runs and other office duties.

The job at Sausalito was funded by a grant, which ran out in 1984. At that time I went to work at the Belvedere Police Department as the Administrative Assistant to the Chief of Police. My duties included taking police reports to the District Attorney's office, assisting officers with their paperwork, and handling the Chief's correspondence and reports.

In the 1980s, Tom had two heart surgeries. The first was at St. Mary's Hospital in San Francisco, in March, 1983. He recovered well from the new valve procedure and was able to go back to work, and to Giants games.

In March, 1985, Tom had bypass surgery at Marin General Hospital. Sadly, Tom never fully recovered from the second surgery. He tried to go back to work, but had to retire from his position as the Cost Accountant at the US Mint. Tom passed away on October 27, 1985.

One good thing did come from his stay at Marin General Hospital: I met one of Tom's nurses, who would become one of my best friends. She was Charlotte Proctor, who, at the time, lived in Corte Madera. Char and I gambled together and traveled together.

In 1989, Char retired from Marin General Hospital, and started working in the health care section at The Redwoods in Mill Valley. The Redwoods is a senior housing area; there are sections for independent living, assisted living, and the health care area.

When she started working there and found out that they were in need of receptionists, Char suggested that I may want to work there, part-time.

Well, part-time it was, until I was 82 years old!

In the 1990s Char and I went on two cruises together. One was to Alaska, and the other to Mexico. During the cruise to Alaska we were upgraded to a stateroom on the top floor of the ship and treated like queens! We also spent our fair share of time in the ship's casino.

When we went to Mexico, we were to meet at Char's house, and my brother Bill was going to take us to the airport in a limo, as he worked at a limo company in Napa. We were wonderfully surprised to find my brother Stan with Bill. Stan had made reservations to go with us to Mexico.

During this voyage, one of our stops was Puerto Vallarta. While off the ship sightseeing, we heard the ship's horns beckoning us back aboard. Hurricane Linda was headed our way! That certainly changed the vacation's itinerary. We were only able to leave the ship again in Ensenada, and, of course, in Los Angeles at the end of the journey.

Char and I at a party.

Knee Injury = Romance

Visiting Bonnie in Palm Desert.

In 1987, while Bonnie was working as a police officer at Twin Cities Police Department, she suffered a knee injury while playing softball. Since she could not work as a patrol officer for a few months, she assisted the detectives with their investigations.

Of course, Bonnie knew all the detectives, but during her time there, she became friendly with one in particular—Sgt. Ray De Leon. Soon they were in Hawaii together, and the rest is history. Ray retired from the department in 1993, and Bonnie has been his best fan, supporting his golf habit ever since.

Due to a back injury, Bonnie had to retire from being a police officer with the Twin Cities Police Department in September, 2000. As luck would have it, the department needed someone who would help with an occasional shift in the dispatch center. For Bonnie, this was perfect. She could work when she wanted, still be "in the mix" at the police department, and earn some spending money. It also gave her the time to travel.

During 2002, Bonnie and Ray purchased a vacation home in Palm Desert, CA, at the Monterey Country Club. Bonnie had her house in Corte Madera, and Ray was in Greenbrae, but Ray wanted to golf in the winter, so off they went. Two years later they sold that house, and bought a brand new house in Indio, California, at Sun City Shadow Hills.

I would fly down to be with them generally three or four times a year—Thanksgiving, my birthday in February, and Easter. During my stays, there were two highlights—being with Bonnie and Ray, and going to a local casino. Would you believe there are five Indian casinos within 30 minutes of Indio? Heaven!

"If I Smoked Again, I Could Die"

Me celebrating my birthday
while working at the Redwoods.

After decades of working, and having been at the Redwoods for 14 years, I decided it was time to retire. I wanted to stay home and take life easy for a while.

In 2005, I took a hard look around the Sausalito house. It needed more work than I had the energy to put into it. We looked around for the perfect place for me.

As I was selling the Sausalito house, "as is," I was buying a two-bedroom condo in Novato, at Villa Entrada, a housing area for seniors. We own our condos, and have a homeowners' association to maintain the homes.

Within months after moving to Novato, I became ill and spent two weeks in the hospital, while 12 pints of "poison" were removed from me. The poison was the buildup of many years of cigarette ingredients; it was removed by a tube through my nose, down to my stomach.

That was a major turning point in my life. After smoking for 70 years, I quit cold turkey! A doctor told me that if I smoked again I could die; that did it for me!

A year later, I had to have my gall bladder removed.

To finish up my health changes after moving to Novato, I had to get my left hip replaced. The operation was supposed to happen in October, 2009, but due to month-long pre-op doctor's orders, I was too weak to be operated on. The doctor had me stop taking most of my daily medicines, and he had me donate two pints of blood!

Three days after having the surgery cancelled—it was cancelled while I was in the hospital on the pre-op gurney—I was receiving blood transfusions to regain my strength.

We tried again on December 10, 2009. Success! From Marin General Hospital, I went to the facility at Smith Ranch Road, San Rafael, CA, to rehab. After three weeks there, including Christmas, Bonnie drove me to the desert.

She and Ray had arranged for me to be in a rehab facility in Rancho Mirage. After a couple of weeks there, I stayed with Bonnie and Ray for a few weeks. Then, I finally got to go back to my own house, and got back to my life.

Bonnie Turned 50

In August, 2009, Bonnie turned 50 years old. Ray, with the assistance of Bonnie's great friend Erin, planned a surprise birthday party for her.

Ray had an even bigger surprise than we could have imagined—he told Bonnie they were getting married ... and the ceremony was going to be the next Friday, September 4!

Ray had all the arrangements made at the Marin County Civic Center. He had arranged for the wedding license, location, and justice of the peace. The ceremony was held on the lawn, outside the Civic Center's cafeteria. There was sunshine, a view, a beautiful fountain, and many friends and relatives. It was a perfect afternoon.

My Brother Ken

Me, my brother Ken, brother Bill, sister Helen, and brother Stan— 2000.

A sad note from 2010—my brother Ken, who lived in Anaheim, passed away.

May I Tell You Something?

On a recent afternoon—September 21, 2012, to be exact—I was at my favorite delicatessen. When I got to the cash register with that day's purchase, there was a gentleman in line ahead of me. He stepped back, and motioned for me to go ahead of him. I told him to please go ahead.

After he bought his food, he stepped back, as if he were waiting for me. I smiled and finished my purchase. The man then said, "I'll place this in your car." I tried to say no, but he was insistent. Instead, I went to the lottery machine to buy a few tickets; as I recall, none bought that day were winners.

As I headed to the door, the gentleman was talking to the cashier. He came back to me and started chatting. He said, "May I tell you something?"

Not knowing what he was thinking, I of course said "Yes."

He looked right at me, and said I would have been a wonderful "gangster's moll." I nearly fainted, but passed it off, telling him I'd missed another opportunity. He escorted me to my car, made sure I was in, closed the door, and gave me a big smile.

The gentleman had been dressed in overalls and a work shirt. He may be a truck driver, stevedore, or something on that order. He had silver hair, a silver beard, and a mustache.

90!

The 90th Birthday Cake!

As I write this, Bonnie and Ray have sold the house in Indio, and we're all in Marin, year-round.

The year 2013 brought my 90th birthday. The exact day, February 6, was a Wednesday. To make it easier for all my friends to help me celebrate, Bonnie and Ray planned a party for me on Saturday, February 9.

The party, a few months in the planning, was at McInnis Park Club Restaurant, on Smith Ranch Road in San Rafael. Bonnie sent out the "save the date" cards and the invitations to my list of friends and family. Some people I hadn't seen in years, and some I had seen in the past week.

I helped with the most important aspect of the party—menu planning!

Bonnie made up poster boards with photos of me throughout my life. She had photos of me as a baby, child, student, worker, traveler, mother, and, of course, an usherette. There were photos of me ushering at the Cow Palace, Winterland and Seals Stadium.

Of course my party had entertainment. During the past few years, we occasionally have lunch at Whistlestop Wheels in San Rafael; Whistlestop Wheels is a bustling senior activities center in San Rafael, housed in an original train station.

One day when we were enjoying lunch, a wonderful crooner named Andrew Clyde was entertaining everyone. Andrew brings his music, his microphone, and his voice—and everyone loves him as he performs the Big Band-era songs.

Bonnie contacted Andrew, and he jumped at being part of our festivities. He walked around singing his beautiful songs as all my guests arrived.

The party was in a private dining area of the restaurant. We had an open bar, balloons, and photos. There were gorgeously set tables for eight; we filled six of those tables with happy guests.

Bonnie, Ray and I greeted all the guests. When we sat down for dinner, the salads and main courses arrived and were enjoyed by all. We had ordered a chocolate birthday cake with chocolate frosting from a local bakery. The restaurant helped by lighting the candles (no, not 90 of them!), and then slicing the cake.

Bonnie and Ray had earlier asked if anyone wanted to say a few words about me. After dinner, some people did speak. I thought, "Here it comes."

Turns out my family and friends were wonderful. I didn't cry—and I did keep smiling through all the nice words. What great honors from my friends and family!

As the evening was ending and my guests began to leave—always with a hug and kiss—I thought, "I am the luckiest girl in the world!"

Two Falls in Two Weeks

February not only had its "ups," it also had its "downs"—two falls I had within two weeks of each other. Though I wasn't badly injured (a bruised rib made me say, "Don't make me laugh!" for a week), it did become more difficult for me to get around, and my doctor said I shouldn't drive any more. Wow, 75 years of practice out the door.

Not horrible, except for getting to the store, doctors' offices, bingo, etc. And what about when my chauffeurs, Bonnie and Ray, go away?

We found one solution when they went to visit friends in the Palm Springs area in April—I spent the week at Aegis in Corte Madera. Aegis is a retirement community area where everyone has their own living area, and you don't have to cook if you don't want to, as there is a great dining room.

Aegis has short-term stays, so folks like Bonnie and Ray can take a little vacation with piece of mind about Mom. I had a lovely studio room with a TV, beautiful shower, private phone line, and a small kitchen area. Their care was wonderful, the three meals a day beautiful, and the coffee nook with fresh coffee, snacks and beautiful desserts was open 24 hours a day!

There was also a weekly calendar with all types of events for everyone to participate in. Live music, bus trips, movies, and Friday Night Happy Hours were among the choices. Even with everything going on at Aegis, you can leave any time you want. There is a driver on staff (for their Cadillac!), your friends can come get you, or, if you drive, you can take yourself out and about.

In my short stay, I became acquainted with very lovely ladies and gentlemen. Nearly every afternoon we'd meet up at the music program of the day. My week drew to an end, with all my pleasant care at Aegis happily remembered. I am back in my own home now. Bonnie and Ray are always here, making sure I'm OK and have enough food!

A Mini High School Reunion

On November 2, 2013 Ray, Bonnie and I attended a memorial service for Ray's former wife, Velma.

Through the years, I had known that Velma's sister, Aurora, was a friend of mine from high school; we graduated from Commerce High School in the same class.

This would be the first time in over 70 years that I would see Aurora. We took to each other right away, talking about school, old boyfriends, and our lives since then.

Bonnie was telling people at the memorial that we were having a "mini high school reunion"… the only two left from our class. Well, I don't know if that is true, but it was a pleasure to see Aurora after all the years. She was so near, yet so far.

Epilogue

And so, for now, with all the adventures and wonderful times I've had, I will close with all my wonderful memories.

I do hope everyone that reads my tales will enjoy them and relive the memories as I have.

This is not "goodbye," just a fond farewell until next time.

My best regards to everyone!

—*Bea*

www.ingramcontent.com/pod-product-compliance
Lightning Source LLC
Chambersburg PA
CBHW050603300426
44112CB00013B/2052